# LEAVING

# FRENCH

## CREEK BAY

ISBN: 978-1-954095-51-9

Cover Photo by Emily Margaret the Authors Daughter
Editor Laurie R. Rouse.

For permission requests, write to the publisher at the address below.

Yorkshire Publishing
1425 E 41st Pl
Tulsa, OK 74105
www.YorkshirePublishing.com
918.394.2665

Published in the USA

THOMAS K. HUNT

# LEAVING FRENCH CREEK BAY

TULSA

ISBN: 978-1-954095-51-9

*Leaving French Creek Bay*
Copyright © 2021 by Thomas K. Hunt
All rights reserved.

Cover Photo by Emily Margaret the Author's Daughter

Editor Laurie R. Rouse

For permission requests, write to the publisher at the address below.

Yorkshire Publishing
1425 E 41st Pl
Tulsa, OK 74105
www.YorkshirePublishing.com
918.394.2665

Published in the USA

I'm dedicating this book to my family and friends that have shown their unconditional love for my life. I am truly blessed to have grown up in one of the most beautiful places in the world with that love and support. I'm writing about what I've experienced. The images of the way life was for me growing up on the river. I'm sure, as you read through this book, you'll find yourself among these pages if you know and love the river as I do.

Thank you all with all my heart. You know who you are.

# Contents

# Leaving French Creek Bay

I see myself on a sunny blue day
Gliding across my river
Leaving French Creek Bay
Smile-filled faces on my left and my right
The sweet smell of the river
The peace that holds me tight
Take me back to the feel of the ease
Fan my face with a cool summer breeze Feel in
your heart for what you see
I see you sitting next to me

I see myself in a clear autumn night
A million stars with the moon shinning bright
Cooler weather just feels so right
Keeping you warm
Holding you tight
Take me back to where I'm me
Show my face for everyone to see
Shed a little light on the family tree
Knowing eyes I'd love to see
I see you sitting next to me

I see myself catching snowflakes on my tongue
Down Manitauk on a long toboggan run

Mitten-covered hands kept warm in the night
Your moonlit eyes shining so bright
The mist of our breath, vapor trails in the light
Take me back to where I need to be
Feeling my life and feeling free
Just one place that I can see
I see you sitting next to me

I see myself on a fresh spring day
The first day the snows gone away
Streams are flowing, the falls falling fast
The kind of day you wish would last
Wafts of lilacs
The slow turn to green
Everything is everywhere and in between
By my river is where I should be
Never missing its journey to the sea
One more thing that I can see
I see you sitting next to me

I see myself on a sunny blue day
Gliding across my river
Leaving French Creek Bay

# Blossoms in the Wind

Blown away like others
Others yet to come
Carried south by a northern wind
Is a son of a Saint Lawrence son

Separated by necessity
Forced to choose another way
Dreaming of the setting sun
Reflecting ambers across the bay

The river lives forever
Perpetual flow of fresh and clean
And like his father before him
He knows what the river means

The innocents of childhood
The wisdom of the old
The beauty in a summer night
The winters long and cold

The simplicity of friendship
Effortlessly taken in
Hearts joined together
From beginning to the end

Buried in the fertile ground
Separated by the known
Family members all laid down
Under rows of faded stones

Each their own gardener
Sowed their seeds to reap more
Blossoms carried with the wind
From roots by the Saint Lawrence shore

# I Remember

I was sitting in a gallery
That's not what it used to be
That was the post office
Years before river rats made cheese

My home, now a restaurant
Witness to the Inlet burning
When flames lit up floating antiques
Monuments from the day
Streamlined, sleek
The face of grace
Testimonies to the trade

Adonis summered in the waves
Hauled from the banks every autumn
While wintering on wooden stilts
Resting until the spring thaw

Evidence is buried or hidden
That was the Catholic school
Those are railroad ties
The water tower was right there

Pictures on a wall hold the truth
Past commanders that held their post

Echoes of colliding glasses
That ended each war story
Blood-red quarters filled the jukebox
That played decades of memories

Black derbies, poles of grease
Fishing ponds behind curtains
Regal Tone music on the block
Real custard from a stand

The grand union of multitudes
Rejoiced in happy hours
Traditional Wednesday filled the lot
Under the shadows of black hills
Mounds of food for the furnaces
Feeding the hungry steamers
Now lay leveled to a park
Where the rails came to an end

# In the Still of the Night

There's a mirror on my river with reflections of light
There's a calm in the evening that holds me tonight
Thoughts all around me seem to dance out of sight
Like silhouettes in the shadows in the still of the night
When I was younger, I smelled the air
Footloose and fancy without any cares
Friends all around me
What a friendship we shared
Friends forever are the echoes I hear
Echoes of laughter, dreams, and fears
Some have remained, some vanished with the years
The weak ones just faded while the strong held tight
As I sit by my river in the still of the night
There's a breeze kicking up now
It steals the calm
The reflections on my river are now all but gone
My thoughts are still dancing with the rhythm of
    the wind
They lead me away to the places I've been
They swirl me and twirl me, and it just feels so right
As I sit by my river in the still of the night

# River Spirits

From Tibbetts Point to the Castle
Life keeps flowing north
From generation to generation
We keep passing the torch

There's mystery in the Islands
From Carlton and beyond Big Round
Folklore and thousands of stories
That have all been handed down

Sunken ships and pirate tales
Ghosts that wonder still
Buried treasure and Indian graves
On Grindstones hallowed hill

A river so deep that no one knows
The depths to which it goes
A river that's so beautiful
Yet so dangerous with its flow

On a blackened night between the lights
Headed in the wrong direction
Many a man has lost his way
And become the rivers possession

Lost souls that still sail the night
Wandering from bay to bay
Bemused spirits drifting along
Still trying to find their way

Yet the river is a dreamland
For both the young and the old
Cool yourself in the summer heat
With fresh clean water and behold

The seductive paradise that traps your soul
Never to let you go
When my time is ended
When my days have ended for me
You'll still find me on my river
Among the spirits sailing free

# Spirit of the River

Hey, stop talking, can't you hear that sound?
The sound of the spirit living here in my town
It floated in on a summer breeze
It looked around and decided not to leave
Buried its bones here before time
Now it lives in each of our minds
It doesn't matter if there's ice and snow
It doesn't matter if the cold winds blow
That spirits deep inside of me
I know it's inside of you
It grabbed us before we knew
There's nothing we can do
It's not a story
It's all true
That spirit's inside of you

It had your father and the fathers before him
They loved the river and the spirit within
Hand me down that
I'll keep it with pride
No generation has the spirit denied
Find me an island
There's thousands to choose
Take your pick, you've got nothing to loose

The spirit lives on each and every one
Under the silver moon
Until the setting sun
So come with me and we'll take a cruise
We can still sing those wintertime blues
Get underneath the golden sun
Ride the wakes for free
You've got the spirit
The spirit's gotten me

Hey, can you hear it
I think you know that sound
The sound of the spirit living here in our town
Sounds of a breeze on a summer night
Safe and warm between red and green lights
Millions of stars fill the sky at night
That's when the spirit shines bright
It's summer, it's time to smile
Take off your shoes
Swim around for a while
Swim with the spirit
It's swimming with you
Keep it warm in the winter
It's the right thing to do
I'm one with the river
The Saint Lawrence Seaway
My roots are nourished from French Creek Bay
The spirit is among us

From the lighthouse passed the span
Behind the smiling eyes of every true friend
On my river under a deep blue sky
If this is heaven
I'm ready to die

# My River and Me

I smell the river
Home is in the air
I see the river
I know I'm there

This river ran through me
It's my turn to oblige
One within its beauty
This river so wide

Crystal springs flowing gently
Whispers peace within my head
Sprinkle me among the crystals
Lay me down in the riverbed

Ashes to ashes
May the dust be blessed
As it turns to silt
In this final rest

Lay me down in my river
Let its life set me free
Flowing on forever
My river and me

# Another Time to Say Good-Bye

I've seen a vision soon to be reality
Fourteen hundred miles from where I am
Once again I'll bathe in the river
In a few more days
I'll be home again

Mother's eyes will be smiling
Three to add to one to make four
The true love of my being
Rests on the Saint Lawrence shore

The celebration of family
The very essence of who you are
Faces around a candlelit table
Glowing in the light of the stars

Sister 'n' aunts, daughters 'n' mothers
Sons 'n' fathers, nephews 'n' brothers
Separated by miles but together in heart
Live with the pain of living apart

Friends that are forever
Smiles that don't lie
Once a year is better then never
For the chance to be eye to eye

The days move like minutes
When I'm home I watch them fly
Time to pack another memory
Another time to say good-bye

# My Home

Birds have flown south with the last fall breeze
Bright leaves of autumn are scattered from trees
As winter slowly steals the green
Clean crisp air surrounds us
We pull our coats in tight
We scurry through the shortest days
We prepare for the longest nights
Soon the river will be frozen
A constant in the circle of its life
Closing the gap between the islands
Brought together by fields of white
A portrait laid out on nature's canvas
A vision of beauty seen with any eye
The nights are cold but warming
As you gaze at the star-filled sky
There is peace and solitude in my paradise
My roots from there still grow
Among the snow, wind, and ice
Will always be my home

# River of Life

Hold me close
As your clean coldness surrounds me
Like an aura of calm

Glide me through your womb
Let me feel your life
Like a mother's love

Let me drink from your vastness
Nourish me with your body
Quench my thirst for life

Cleanse me with your freshness
Like an oak leaf in the autumn dew
Shining in the morning sun

Carry me down
Float me with your current
Following the sun to your western edge

Give me your life
Let me swim in your wonderment
Forever flow gentle in my mind

# Reflections

Mirrors are made to last
They don't hold images of the past
The reflection from where I am
Is all you can see from where I've been
Take a look into the glass
Looks like it's looking at you
See the green of the grass
The oranges and the blues
You want it to last
What's the right thing to do?
You don't have to ask
It's all laid out in front of you
Reflections on the river
What's up is also down
In the still of the silence
In the calm of my town
Whistling crickets are all you hear
Maybe the hum of an outboard coming around the pier
There's no other place like this
On this moonlit night
Beside this fire
In my hometown tonight

Sit back and laugh
Cry when you need to
Make each day last
They've been given to you
Reflections so beautiful to see
The beauty of the sky brought down to its knees
Taking your mind to where it should be
Smiling all the way because you're happy
What's up is also down
Reflections on the river in my hometown
Sitting back in my Adirondack
Admiring the view
The campfire smoke and the crisp, clean air
Smells so right to you
Keep your palm trees and your sand
That's no life for me
Give me tall pines on the land
Give me the river and white birch trees
There's no other place like this on earth
Under this moonlit night
Reflections in this glass-covered river
In my hometown tonight
Mirrors are made to last
They don't hold images of the past
The reflection from where I am
Is all you can see from where I've been

# Hold Me Close in the Night

Shroud me with a blanket of stars
Hold me close in the night
There's a reason I've come this far
This is what I'm trying to write

I can't escape this fertile soil
My roots are strong and deep
My time is limited between my toil
I gather up all I can reap

The road is long but a familiar one
I've traveled it many times
It leads me to the river
Where I can rest my mind

A summer breeze in the midday sun
The sound of laughter in the air
A feeling of content when the day is done
Remembering days without a care

Please steal me away, don't let me go
I won't put up a fight
Keep me here forever more
Hold me close in the night

# I Long to Be in the Islands

I work on the Arthur Kill
Pulling boom for oil spills
It ain't bad work, and I kinda like the pay
But the air is dirty, and the water is black
Oh, Mamma, won't you take me back
To that place on the river right off of French Creek Bay

Oh, I long to be in the islands because it's summer time
Summer always has a way of taking me home
I'll pack my bags, and I'll be on my way
Say good-bye to Jersey for a couple of days
Get on that highway
Clayton bound

It's always nice to come home
It's good to see my good old friends
It's such a nice feeling
I wish it would never end
But I work on the Arthur Kill
And I'll be back to oil spills

It ain't bad work, and I kind a like the pay
But the air is dirty, and the water is black
You know my heart will be back
On the Saint Lawrence River right off of French
Creek Bay

# Loving Memories

Loving memories of smiling faces
People with smiling faces have the hearts to fill
the world
Smiles come from the heart
We should plant our smiles before they disappear
We need beautiful smiles to blossom every year
Nickel candy at the corner store
You know the one I'm talking about
Everything that was near was far
I could call you with just a shout
We'd yell, "Gun it," to the captains then we'd jump
right in
Rode that backwash down the river for another spin
Laid back and enjoyed the thrill of those rides
We did it right there off of Riverside Drive
It was the center of the world
Right there where Mary meets John
Close your eyes and picture that time
Go on travel back in your mind
The innocent days enjoyed so many ways
Just the thought should bring a smile
I'm sure you're smiling right now
Smiling of a thought you haven't thought for a while

Kicking hard to reach the sky
Little faces in the sun
Minds full of the whys
Surrounded by a river of fun
It doesn't matter of the time
It's there to cross the mind
It's always been on track
Creating memories to bring smiles back
Think back to when you stood there to
There's been more then a time or two
You may be traveling or you may be right there
Dig up a smile go on and share
No matter how far you roam
No matter how far you've gone
It's still the center of the world
Right there where Mary meets John
Bring back your own memory
Share some smiles between you and me
We'll plant them before they turn to frowns
Before you know it they'll be planted all around
They'll grow just like the tall pine trees
Smiles from the loving memories

# The Seasons

Summer days have faded
June, July, and August a distant dream
Golden rays, blue skies, misty summer steam
Surrounding greens, morning blankets of dew
Fields of wild flowers suffuse the rainbows hue
The soothing river, cool velvet on the skin
Sounds of laughter from children jumping in
Street corner bustle, music in the air
Roller coasters and smells from a fair
Those days are gone
They've all disappeared
Now that fall has fallen
Autumn's fallen here
Browns and reds, yellows and gray
Cool breezes getting cooler every day
Pepper allies, bonfires with rising flames
Cheers and chants the night before the game
Sweater weather, apple cider from jars
The fullest moons encircled by stars
Dusky dawn's rise through colorless haze
Clouded skies, overcastting days
Gradient temperatures sloping down
Turning dew to frost that covers the ground

Soon to be shrouded under depths of frozen white
Cold and crisp are the breath shown nights
Ice sickles hang jagged in rows
Evergreen wreaths don crimson bows
Fat men of white guard frozen lawns
Three-toed footprints freshly made in the dawn
Ice sickles wither, shedding their tears
The frozen snow will soon disappear
Waterfalls flow forceful with might
Crystal-clean foaming bubbles of white
Browns turn to green, trees sprout their buds
The sun warms the earth and dries up the mud
Sweet smell of lilacs waft through the night
A red-breasted robin makes her first flight
April showers cleanse the land clear
Once again springtime is here
It won't be long for it to will end
Summer days will be back again

# Autumn in Clayton

Step in the breeze
At summers end
It's your favorite time
It's fall again

Put on a sweater
Maybe wear a hat
Time for the witch's cat
Everything's golden, yellow, and red
A pile of leaves
Make a colorful bed

Distant cheers from a football field
The hero scores, and his fate is sealed
Once in glory
A small taste of fame
That's not his story
He just loved the game

Every year you live for this chill
The one that falls
Over McCarn Hill

The echoing burst
From a blind that has sight

So many fly away
To rest their wings at night

It's not a season
But a feeling inside
A full, bright moon
Fills the night sky
Millions of stars
Diamonds of light
Autumn in Clayton
On an October night

# Autumn Has Fallen

The sky traverse with gray and soft white light
Lay quilted as far as the eye
The chill slow dances with the wind
Embraced so close as if were one
The brightly colored leaves
Play tag and chase each other
In the cool breeze
Before landing for their final rest
Waiting to be entombed
By a pall of crystal white

Autumn has fallen
Overtaking the summer
That now fades to memory
Of blues and bright yellows
Of warmth and hurried motion
Of hot bodies cooled
By the clean river springs

Autumn has fallen
Stomping and pushing down the degrees
With each passing day
Stealing the long, lighted days
Now cut short by early dusk

And dampened dawns
The moon at its fullest
Shines brilliant against the nights darkened sky
Autumn has fallen
Another summer has said good-bye

# The Colors of Fall

Lost in the tropics of continuous green
Not complaining mind you
It's a beautiful scene
But on this day my thoughts are adrift
Of the sight I would see as I sat on my cliff
A Northern boy bred and pure
Camped on a hill so high for sure
Deep in the fall and far from others
I'd sit alone and gaze at the colors
Bright yellows, oranges, reds, and browns
All surrounding my quaint little town
Cool autumn breezes fell across my face
I'd sit for hours in my private high place
Every year you could find me there
If you climbed my hill, if you dared
But here on this October day
As my mind has gone astray
So many years since I've sat so high
And seen the autumn's beauty in my eyes
Now the palm trees cast no shade
The only breezes are winds of trade
But every year around this time
The colors of fall fill my mind

# I Know I'm Way Back When…

I know I'm way back when among the loving known,
I know I live among them, in hearts where I call home
In this place that holds me tight
Buried roots under northern lights
Memories that live inside
Reappear then run and hide
Shaded faces that reveal the kind
Held warmly in the mind
A feeling seen through smiling eyes
Touches the soul and you know why

I know I'm way back when among the loving kind
I know I live among them in thoughts that pass
    their minds
In this place that holds me tight
Tiny glimpses of every night
Feelings felt and sights seen
Everything is everything
Still there, though miles away
Still there, but in a different way
Sending thoughts in the still of the night
Just in time for the morning light

I know I'm way back when among the loving known,
I know I live among them, in hearts where I call home
In this place that holds me tight
Youth-spent days and teen-filled nights
Following footprints on hallowed ground
Scattered pieces left all around
Featured faces bring back the past
Subtle reminders of those that have passed
Live on through the knowing kind
Passed on to another mind

I know I'm way back when among the loving kind,
I know I live among them in thoughts that pass
    the mind
I know I'm way back when among the loving known,
I know I live among them, in hearts where I call home

# That Boy

Avoiding all the shadows
Moving with the sun
Searching all the landscapes
Searching for some fun

Endless days in the summer haze
Running wild and free
How I long for those golden days
And to find that boy in me

The river ran through my veins
So clean and cool and clear
Dancing barefoot in the rain
So innocent without a fear

I could be anything
A fool without a care
But I lost him along the way
That boy who lived there

Days between the islands
Nights under the moon
How I long for that time again
When the days moved slower in June

Now miles separate me
Many years have robbed my time
The scenery is not the same
In the landscapes of my mind

The reality is just a memory
Of the sun and fun and joy
And the lazy, hazy summer days
When I was that boy

# Summer Rain

An army of raindrops marches across the river
Sending out sprinkles to scout the way
Within minutes, darkness overtakes us
Heavy rain wets the day

Lightning flashes in bolts that streak
Thunder crashes in its wake
Sheets of pearls bounce on the streets
Gutters flood with all they can take

Trees bend in its fury
Their leaves shine with wet
People run in a scurry
Avoiding puddles without success

Barefooted children prance and dance
Heads back, mouths open wide
Drink in the tears from heaven
While they're told to get inside

As quick as it had started
It's over with a calm
The freshness wafts the air
A summer rain has come and gone

# Song of the River

Long ago
Next to my window in the night
I'd find my bed and lie down
Turn my head just right
To listen for the river song

Flowing within its rhythm
A wave crashes with a rock
A bass breaks the surface
A lone goose trails his flock

Some midnight cruiser
Heading for home
Hear the hum of his engine
A fading pitch tone

The roll of the lakers
Keeps the beat along the way
Two pass each other in stereo
Then the horns begin to play

A peaceful, easy feeling
Yes that's another song
But your senses get reeling
This is where you belong

The melody of the river
Is free and there for you
Just turn down your volume
Let that symphony come through

As for me, I'll bide my time
Keep dreaming of the day
To hear the song of the river
That river shore can play

# I'll Take That Walk Again

We were there in the beginning
Pieces still remain
The eyes see the loss
The heart pays the cost
While nothing remains the same

We used to walk along the tracks
Warmed by the soft summer sun
Lie down in a deep bed of grass
When the day was done

Blanketed by the stars at night
Lost in true content
Those were the years of innocence
Those years were heaven sent

Running wild, full of freedom
Made right choices alone the way
A smile forms from just a thought
When I drift back to those days

Chances taken mistakes made
With fun along for the ride
A beautiful beginning
That can never be denied

Flying high behind the pilots mask
Hoping for a smooth flight
Careful with your landing
You don't want to crash tonight

Lost among the islands
With everywhere to go
Everywhere you look
You see someone you know

Though the tracks are long gone
I'll take that walk again
Lay myself in the tall grass
Beside a lifelong friend

# Sweet Dream Memories

Now and then I need to get away
Travel my mind far from my day
When I need a place to go
Sweet dream memories make it so

There is a town just south of Ontario
It sleeps by the river under a blanket of snow
It's so easy to exist without a care
When you are young and growing there

Crystal springs sparkle clean with shine
Full moon rising over tall green pines
A peaceful silence wafts the still nights
Holds you in comfort close and tight

An amber field of grass and weeds
Rolls like waves in the autumn breeze
A hawk in flight with a watchful eye
Slowly circling the midday sky

A well-known dog asleep in the shade
Flying papers on the street from a parade
A boy on the bank with a line in the river
The warmth of a fire that steals your shiver

There is a town just south of Ontario
All my days of growing were there
That's the place where I need to go
Sweet dream memories make it so

# The Porch

Born and raised on the Saint Lawrence River
Respectfully proud of what's been given
Sitting by our river caught in this peaceful calm
Watching the colors of the day fade with the sun
Quiet souls surround us
We see the same that they have seen
We've seen it all through different eyes
Our blood is from their being
Sit on this porch
Light another torch
Show me another sun
Shine on this life of mine where the river runs
Spend the day with your nose in the air
Only to smell that fresh clean air
Set your smile free and watch it run
Run across the river in the summertime fun
Sitting by our river caught in this peaceful calm
Watching the colors of life fade with another days sun
Sitting here resting at day's end
Truly content with all our river friends
The roots run deep
We share what we reap
It's the only way

We'll live on the Saint Lawrence until our dying day
The river nights are a sacred time
It's all in the frame of the mind
It's something that is real
There's something that you feel
So sit on this porch
Light another torch
We're going to have our fun
Just this side of French Creek Bay
Where the river runs
Raise your glass
Drink from a flask
Let's have another round
Under this river moon tonight
On the best porch in this town

# The First Snow

The crispness of Saturday morning
with Autumn now a dream
Frozen crystal feathers on the
pane form a wintry scene
Escaping the warmth of my blankets I'd
skate across that cold wooden floor
Waking all the others as I darted past their doors

I'd run for the door without a thought
and my mom would get so mad
Get in here right now mister
before I get your dad
The first snow had fallen and
I couldn't feel the cold
Outside in my pajamas now I
understand her scold

I couldn't wait to get ready as I
opened the closet in the hall
All my winter coverings smelled
of musk and old mothballs
My mittens on a string to lace

through my woolen coat
My scarf around my neck to keep
the chill off of my throat
Snow pants in my boot tops to
keep me warm and dry
My mom would put my hat on last
right down to the top of my eyes

In a flash, I was out that door whirling
in that white powder fluff
Laughing with every tumble,
man I just loved that stuff
Rolling three giant snowballs each one bigger
than the next to form our yards guardian
He was better than all the rest

We'd grab our sleds and saucers
and head for Manitauk Hill
The rich kids had toboggans and
for one of those I'd kill
Sledding down that mountainside
as far as I could go
Lost within my winter fun so
thankful for that snow

When the day was over just before my time to go
I'd lie down in a cloud of white to
form an angel in the snow
With rosy cheeks and runny nose,
I'd yell out, "mom I'm home"
I'd get undressed and warm myself with
hot cocoa and marshmallow foam

# It's Wintertime Again

The air holds tight the chilling cold that bites
 uncovered skin
Crisp and clean fragrance hold
It's wintertime again
The moon hides from everything
No stars are overhead
Degrees driven down by the factor
Heavy snow clouds begin to shed
Pelts of white encase the fall
Now buried is the withering brown
From the north come violent squalls
That whistle through this town
Gusts hit like a fist form virgin drifts
It's a beautiful sight to see
Tall pines donned with white lace veils
Dance for the white birch trees
A quilt of cloud spread across the sky
Blankets the frozen vast
A field of white stretched before my eyes
Pictured memories developed to last
Autumn has fallen beneath her right hand friend Gone
are the colors of October
It's wintertime again

# Winter in Clayton Has Begun

The snow-covered ice illuminates with white as the
  moon shines over the river
Shanties cast black shadows from random settings
Drifts form snow waves that stretch out across the bay
  under Luna's grace
Around the corner, buoys take rest at their winter height
Resting on the dock where the rails came to an end
Where hills of black coal fed the furnaces, keeping crews
  afloat and the chill from our homes
Red and green, red and green all in a row
Oversized seasonal ornaments stand in contrast to
the winter's landscape
No longer flashing their beacons of light across the river
  that's now turned to ice
Appear more beautiful than expected as they stand
  guard along our riverside bank
It's winter in Clayton

The size of the snowflakes seen best with the backlight
  of the street lamps
Trenches plowed for passageways where the walls grow
  higher with each passing snowfall
Snow angels formed by children close to heaven
Sending signals to reach their guardians

The return of the snowmen
They come to spend the winter
Keeping watch at their frozen post with coal-filled eyes
Waiting for the thaw to become one with the river
Warm souls, smiles on faces
Lost in the smile of a friend having fun
Time now for one of those face-to-faces
Winter in Clayton has begun

# Underneath Our Northern Sky

I'm sending you this photograph
It's me looking back at you
Thought it would bring a smile
Seventy-six, two months past June
Look deep within the photo
Deep within the eyes
See the content that lies there
Underneath my Northern sky
Happy in my red Hawaiian
Slightly buzzed and feeling high
Played with innocence among the islands
Underneath my northern sky
Faces still remain there
Smiling eyes that have seen me cry
Souls that really do care
Live underneath my northern sky
Roots of deep grown memories
Living deep behind the eyes
Fragments of another time
Underneath my northern sky
You'll see me smile
You won't have to try
On the river with a friend

Underneath our northern sky
Look deep within the photograph
Know that life behind the eyes
Know the reason you possess it
Underneath our northern sky
I hope you get this photograph
Just once may it pass your eyes
It was taken just for you
Underneath our northern sky
Let that smile surround you
I'll shed another tear and cry
Tell the world over breakfast
Underneath our northern sky

# Where I Need to Be

One road leads and branches into three
You can take the left or right
The middle road is the road for me
Place me in the center tonight
Right where Mary crosses John
Under the stars and a moonlit night
Someone turned the northern lights on
It was a beautiful sight
Rock me gently roll me slow
Feel that summer breeze blow
Waking up in the morning sun
Basking in its glow
Drifting as the river runs
Not caring where I go
Walking through the autumn
An explosion of color
Nature's portrait of life
A landscape like no other
Taste, smell, and feel the first frost
Take me to my river
Let me leap in the ice and snow
Blind me in the white
May the north winds blow

Warmed by a fire to chase the chill away
Lost on my river for another winter's day
Lost on my river
Knowing right where I am
On the bank of the Saint Lawrence
Standing with a lifelong friend
The river holds me
It's where I want to be
When I'm on my river
I'm am truly me
Only in my dreams
I seem to find my way
Only in my mind
I lay back and drift away
One day you'll find me
Right where I need to be
Lost on my river
That's where you'll find me

# Watching Sprouts Blossom

Blue herons calling out
Greet the break of dawn
A newborn whitetail
Suckling a lying fawn
A barking dog spreading his scent
A warning boundary
A line of his defense
The smell of the river
The sound of its flow
Gentle waves caressing the banks below
Another day on the river
Born and bred in its way
The river flows through us
Let it flow for one more day
A slow cruise to somewhere
You can feel it in the air
There are spirits here among us
You can feel them everywhere
Anticipation is part of the cruise
A belief in a belief
The right to choose
In waist-high-level water
Toes buried in the sand

Wearing your warmest smile
Wading with the best of friends
Baptized by this water
Out beyond this sacred beach
We talk about the party
We practice what we preach
Loving and sharing
Enjoying the way it should be
Watching sprouts bloom on the family tree
Soul mates by the dozens
Under the shining sun
Immediate family, friends, and cousins
Watching the river run
Known blessings of where we are
Under the comfort of a blanket of stars
We drift ourselves home
Back with smiling eyes
Say goodnight and dream
Wake to the river sunrise
We show up in our bodies
We've paid the dues
Our souls will follow
They're all paid up too
When the last one moves over
The next one appears
The love of tradition year after year
We'll meet at Potter's

Lay back and have fun
Drink to ourselves until we're done
Share the laughter and shout out cheers
From time to time, there's tears in the beer
History in the making
Teaching what is known
Caring for the crops
Back to the first seed sown
Loving and sharing
Enjoying the way it should be
Watching sprouts blossom on the family tree

# The River Still Flows Through

Here's a little something I'm sure you'll relate
About the river that flows north from a lake
When you hear this, I know you'll agree
This is the place for you and me
The beautiful Saint Lawrence flows
It runs through this northern land
Flowing through so many souls
I see now was nature's plan
Her waters surround a sacred place
To live there, you would know
Nourished in the fresh, clean air
The soil's rich, and the roots take hold
Baptized in her waters
She then flowed within my soul
As she does with all the others
Strays who still call it home
I wish I was on the edge
Standing on her shore
If that wish did come true
I wouldn't wish for anything more
Bathe me in her cool springwaters
Let me walk her frozen path
Passed down from sons and daughters

From the legends of their past
All the children know the feel
From the river where they got their start
I know now that you agree
This place holds your heart
I wish I were there sitting next to you
I remember you from a younger day
I remember the smile in your eyes
I remember you no other way
We knew that was the place
We knew it from the start
We could see it in each other's face
We still feel it in our hearts
Living under circumstance
Forced to be on the roam
Longing for that day to come
The day we make it home
You may get out of the water
But the river still flows through
No matter where you go, my friend
The river's going to flow through you

# Can You Imagine

Can you imagine?
There was a day
When no more than a canoe cut through this river
A native man on his native land
A Tuscarora paddling the river he called the Kahnawá'kye
Meaning to him big waterway
Can you imagine?
Imagine it back then?
The beauty of this river
Virgin soil untouched by man
I imagine that native smiling
Living in the paradise of the Thousand Islands
The evergreens, the deer, the bear
The foul abundant everywhere
The river fed all the need
It was the center of his world
It was all the world he knew
To him it was everything
Everything was good
Can you imagine?

# Home Again

I can smell my youth as I come down from the hill
Now the river's in my eyes
This place holds me still
The streets are the same in this old, familiar place
I'm called by name
They still recognize my face
Smiles to the left
Handshakes to the right
Happy in the middle of old friends tonight
The warmth from the comfort
The chill from the fact
The thrill from of it all to hear "Welcome back!"

# A Lifelong Friend
# Just Reappeared

A lifelong friend just reappeared
He came from out of the blue
We reminisced about our old friends
We reminisced about you
He came and sat beside me
It was great to see my old friend
Then softly said, "It's nice to see you again"
He smiled and sat back in his grin
All at once he took me back
Back to the innocence of the days
On the streets of Clayton where we laughed and played
I was glad to see him
I was grateful for the time
Then the alarm clock sounded off
Stealing him from my mind.
"Captain Paul, do come back
You're welcome anytime
Bring back those sweet memories
The ones that wait in my mind
We have so many tales to tell
Seems there wasn't enough time in our time

I'll drift off and wait for you
Wait for that grinning smile
When you come back, wear your captain's hat
This time stay for a while
We swam in the beach off Mary at the bottom of
the hill
Yelled no chips on windows before swinging for the
knitting mill
Lived through winter freezes waiting for the warmth
of spring
We enjoyed our innocence
We enjoyed everything
Summer opened up our lives with the river so wide
Lost in our world of pretend
Not knowing we had to survive
Through the colorful falls we shared it all
Our motto, 'Friends to the end'"
A lifelong friend just reappeared
He brought it all back for me to see
I woke up, and he disappeared
That was Captain Paul and me

# I Know It's an Antique

Through beers and tears
Through card-filled night
They played their games, but in the morning light
They were back at their trade, making them right
The way they ride through the river is such a
    beautiful sight
They made something from the right thing
They made them sturdy and strong
They knew what would happen
Avoided what could go wrong
They built them together
Then others came around
These were the boat builders in our town
They made them slick and fast
They made them long and lean
We know they made them to last
They are living testimonies
Do you just cruise around?
Do you still go for speed?
I know it's an antique
It looks so polished and sleek
They knew what they were doing
They understood the need

They built them for pleasure
Not one thought of greed
They did it right
They're still holding tight
They don't make them like that anymore
You can watch the parade in the midday sun
From the banks of the Saint Lawrence shore
Sit back easy, go as you go
In your mind, you already know
You're going to throw that throttle
You're going to let that beauty fly
Out of respect, you're always going to try
They'd be proud to know how we show their pride
Who knows, maybe they're along for the ride
I'm glad that they were around
They were the boat builders in our town

# Another Christmas

Another Christmas under this palm tree
Something that never seemed right
Here I am once again missing family and friends
On this hot December night
I have love all around me, as well as do all of them
Once again it's that time of year
Another Christmas we're not together again
Still we're all smiling, enjoying life tonight
That's the way it should be
Thinking as one on this holy night
Waking up on Christmas morning
There was nothing like it
Cutting loose, heading for that tree
There was nothing like it to me
All the hearts were opened
Love shared with company
It felt like Christmas
It was the best feeling to me
Smiling faces everywhere
Handmade Nativity scenes
An innocent time that still lives in my mind
I still feel what that joy can bring
Another Christmas under this palm tree

It's never ever felt right
Everything green is covered with lights
I prefer backdrop white
Give me that crisp, cool northern air
The smell of wood smoke in the night
At this time of the year, I see the same, old sight
Another year of me being here missing family
and friends
Together yet apart in the end
On Christmas once again

# Underneath Our Blue

Eyes open in the pallid
Gone is the shine
Lost are the days of color
Kept is this dream of mine
A dream fills my head
Smooth bed of green
Beside our beautiful river
Water crystal clean
Home is my surroundings
The sky the bluest blue
I am again nineteen
Again nineteen with you
A dream of the deepest
Not knowing what is meant
Vivid smiles, passing thoughts
Jasmine without scent
Here on the other side
This other side with you
Living in your light
Underneath our blue
Love within your smile
Knowing you're the one
Feeling you inside me

Sharing golden sun
Then the dream escapes me
Blue turns to gray
I know I dream in color
I live without it every day
Then calm among the shadows
It's rest that I will find
Roll back in the colors
To this dream of mine
Fall back to innocence
Running back to you
Bathe again in crystal clean
Underneath our blue

# The Last Time I Saw Her

Her last sunset over the islands
Descending over the Canadian sky
Her pain had finally lifted
She spread her wings to fly
The saline trails had all dried up
There were no more tears to cry
She gently closed her tired eyes as she said her last
good-bye
The l ast t ime t hat I  s aw her, we were down a t the
old hotel
A smile fell across her face as we dipped into the well
We reminisced of days gone by
We shared a tear or two
She said she hoped to see me the next time I
passed through
I heard she made her way down South
She found some new sunshine
Hooked up with a long-lost friend
I heard everything was fine
They tied the knot and were on their way
They had a baby girl
Everything was going great as they stepped into
their world

We lost touch as the years flew by
Separated by more than a mile
Her image living in my mind always brought a smile
Then in a dream so vivid she passed me in the night
All day long she was on my mind
Something didn't feel right
That's the day I got the call
I held that phone to my ear
A piece of me died right there from the news that I
    would hear
I walked out in the morning sun
I thought about our time
I thought about her smiling face and the peace now she
    would find

# Circle of Life

Summer passed undetected
Pushing itself into autumn causing it to fall
It didn't fall here
Autumn never falls here in the land of the palms
I've been to a place where autumn falls
I've seen emblazoned backdrops of life
Resplendent explosions of nature
Accompanied by soft, cool breezes
Bearing aromas of ripened fruits and redolent flowers
Where the moon casts the biggest and brightest
    silver shine
Glistening across the river
Making shadows of the tall pines
Sweaters drawn tight
Cool but not cold
Yet turning colder with each day
Witnessing the gradual decaying of beauty
Soon to be barren of foliage
Colorless grays doomed to fill the days light
Sit watch over orchards of skeleton trees
Time will soon be frozen to the ground
Buried under drifts of blinding white

Subzero crystal rain is woven together that blankets
    the quilted landscape
Extended days drag themselves into one another The
air bitter, biting and cutting at dried flesh Chapped
smiles   in   temporary   sanctuaries   from
    the elements
Try to heal themselves under smears of wax
Cracks are easy to find when they run along pallid hide
The warmth sought soon turns to fever
Spreading like the plague from cabin to cabin Locked
away, imprisoned in the mind is the perpetual
    though of spring
The vernal equinox
Nature's rebirth
As old as the ages of time that once again will bequeath
    itself to summer
Completing the circle for yet another revolution

# To Last for All Time

I've opened up my soul, my heart, my mind
Poured them onto pages to last for all time
Deep within myself my thoughts, I clearly see
It's time to bring them out
It's time to set them free
Visions stored in my mind's eye float across the pages
I watch them fill the empty sheets
Recording my different stages
Some have brought real pleasure, while others
    were unkind
Some have shown the truth
That's been hard to find
Don't judge the author
No labels needed here
No harm was ever meant
No one should ever fear
It could be the proxy
For the ending of my name
A slow-burning fire that's sure to lose its flame
Here it is for all to see
This life that I call mine
Laid out in black and white
To last for all time